Science of Skill Acquisition

The 30 Days Game Plan

Jagriti International Publications Pvt. Ltd.

A Constituent Unit of Jagriti Sansthan

Dr. Yogesh Kumar

Professor, TMCON, Teerthanker Mahaveer University,
Moradabad, UttarPradesh. 244001

This Textbook is Dedicated to all the enthusiatic professionals.

To every curious soul who was told,

"You're not talented enough."

May this book remind you:

You don't need to be born with it, you can build it.

Keep learning. Keep growing.

Contents

Foreword

In a world that moves faster with each passing day, the ability to learn new skills, quickly and effectively, is no longer a luxury. It's a necessity.

This book is more than just a collection of techniques or advice. It is an invitation to break free from the old myths about talent and intelligence. Through this structured 30-day approach, Dr. Yogesh Kumar guides you to understand that mastery is not a matter of luck, but of process, mindset, and focus.

Whether you want to learn a language, master a musical instrument, write with clarity, or develop leadership skills, the principles in this book are designed to unlock the path to success for anyone, at any age.

Consider this book your personal roadmap to self-mastery. Follow it closely, and the results may surprise you.

Shri Devi Singh Dhakad
Director, Jagriti Sansthan

Preface

I wrote this book because I believe that anyone can learn anything, if they are willing to start.

So many of us hold back, trapped by the idea that "some people are just born talented" or that "I'm too old for this now." These beliefs stop more dreams than failure ever could.

Over the years, I've observed one truth: **skill is built, not bestowed.**

This book is the product of both research and real-world experience, a step-by-step plan designed to help you master a new skill in just 30 days. Whether you want to boost your career, enrich your personal life, or simply prove to yourself that you can, the process you'll learn in these pages will transform the way you approach learning, forever.

This is not a book to read and forget. It is a book to use.

I invite you to take the challenge, put these ideas into practice, and witness firsthand how capable you truly are.

Dr. Yogesh Kumar

Acknowledgments

No book is created in isolation.

I am deeply grateful to all the teachers, thinkers, and learners whose questions and insights inspired the ideas in this book. The psychology of learning, the science of habit formation, and the stories of everyday people taking on new skills have shaped this work from start to finish.

A special thanks to my friends, family, and colleagues who encouraged me to put these thoughts on paper, and to the readers, present and future, who will carry this journey forward by daring to learn something new.

This book is inspired by:

- The countless creators, makers, teachers, and learners who prove every day that human potential is limitless.

- The wisdom of researchers like Anders Ericsson, Carol Dweck, and James Clear, whose work shapes how we understand learning, habit formation, and mastery.

- And finally, to you, the reader, for choosing to believe in progress over perfection, and for showing up even when it felt uncomfortable.

Every great skill begins with a single choice:

"I'm willing to start."

To the curious minds: this book is for you.

Introduction

Have you ever watched someone effortlessly play a song on a guitar, speak a new language, code an app, or lead a team, and thought, "I wish I could do that, but I'm just not talented enough"?

I'm here to tell you: **you are wrong**.

Skill is not something you are born with. It's something you build, day by day.

The problem isn't that you lack talent. The problem is that traditional education has misled you into believing that learning must be slow, painful, and only for the gifted few. In reality, learning is faster, easier, and more accessible than ever, if you approach it the right way.

This book will show you how.

Inside these chapters, you'll find a simple formula for mastering any skill in 30 days. You'll learn how to break down big goals, how to structure your practice, how to handle setbacks, and, most importantly, how to prove to yourself that you are capable of growth at any age.

This is more than a book. It's a challenge.

If you're ready to rewrite the story you tell yourself about learning, let's begin.

1: The 30-Day Promise

Why 30 Days?

Think about how fast a month goes by. In 30 days, you celebrate a birthday, pay a few bills, binge a series, or scroll through hundreds of social media posts. But what if, instead of letting 30 days drift by, you used them, intentionally, to transform a part of yourself? This is not about becoming world-class in 30 days. This is about laying a solid foundation, breaking inertia, and gaining momentum toward true mastery.

30 days is long enough to build a habit, yet short enough to feel doable. It's a window where your brain, routine, and energy can align toward something new, exciting, and empowering.

The Power of Intentional Learning

Most people "hope" to learn something new. They dabble, browse a few articles, maybe buy a course, and stop halfway. Mastery doesn't happen by accident, it's a product of consistent, focused effort.

When you decide to master a skill in 30 days, you make a shift from passive wishing to active doing. You set goals, track progress, and overcome excuses.

Skill Selection: The First Big Decision

Before we dive into the how, you need to choose your *what*. The key is to pick a skill that meets three criteria:

1. **Motivating**: You're genuinely excited to learn it.

2. **Measurable**: You can clearly see progress.

3. **Manageable**: You can realistically practice it daily for the next 30 days.

Some examples:

- Learn conversational Spanish

- Play five songs on the guitar

- Build your first mobile app

- Run 5km without stopping

- Create and launch a blog

- Learn to cook 10 healthy meals

This book will give you a framework that works for almost *any* skill. You don't need talent, just time, commitment, and a smart plan.

The Mindset of a 30-Day Master

Let's get one thing straight: Mastery isn't magic. It's not reserved for "gifted" people or those with endless time. It's about attitude. Here's the mindset you'll need:

- **Progress over perfection**

- **Consistency over intensity**

- **Curiosity over comparison**

- **Reflection over repetition**

You'll stumble, get stuck, and maybe even want to quit. That's normal. The goal is not to *avoid* failure, it's to *outgrow* it.

The 30-Day Formula (Preview)

Here's what you'll be learning in this book:

1. **Day 1–3**: Define your why, clarify your skill, break it into sub-skills

2. **Day 4–10**: Set daily goals, build routines, gather tools

3. **Day 11–20**: Deep practice, feedback loops, momentum-building

4. **Day 21–29**: Refinement, real-world application, reflection

5. **Day 30**: Celebrate progress, review, plan for what's next

Your First Action Step

Take 10 minutes after reading this chapter and write down the answer to this:

> **"If I could master any skill in the next 30 days, what would it be and why?"**

Pick something that excites you, something that would mean something if you could say "I did that in just one month."

You're not just learning a new skill, you're learning how to learn. That's a superpower.

2. The Science of Skill Acquisition

Why Do Some People Learn Faster?

You've probably met people who seem to "pick things up" instantly. Whether it's learning a new language, mastering a software tool, or nailing a new recipe, they make it look easy.

It's not luck. It's not genetics.

It's strategy.

Decades of research in cognitive psychology and neuroscience show that rapid learners use specific techniques. They know how to:

- Break complex skills into smaller chunks.
- Focus deeply during short, structured practice sessions.
- Use feedback loops to correct mistakes fast.

And the best part? You can apply the same principles.

The Four Stages of Learning

Whenever you learn something new, your brain moves through these predictable stages:

1. **Unconscious Incompetence**
   ("I don't know what I don't know.")
   At the start, you're unaware of how much you don't know. This is the blind spot phase.
2. **Conscious Incompetence**
   ("I know what I don't know.")
   Here you recognize the gaps in your knowledge. Frustrating but vital.
3. **Conscious Competence**
   ("I know what to do, but I have to think about it.")
   Practice makes you better, but it still requires effort and focus.

4. Unconscious Competence
("I just do it.")
The skill becomes automatic. Think: tying your shoes or driving.

Your goal in 30 days is to move from stage 1 to stage 3 or even close to 4, depending on the complexity of the skill.

The Power of Focused Practice

Malcolm Gladwell popularized the idea that 10,000 hours are needed for mastery. But here's the catch:
It's not about the hours. It's about how you use them.

Deliberate practice: not just "doing" the skill, but practicing in a way that stretches your abilities, invites feedback, and focuses on weak spots, is what turns hours into real progress.

In this 30-day journey, your practice will be:

- **Purposeful:** Each session has a goal.

- **Timed:** 30 to 90 minutes of deep, distraction-free focus.

- **Reviewed:** Adjusted based on what worked and what didn't.

Neuroplasticity: Your Brain's Superpower

The brain is not static. It rewires itself based on what you practice. Scientists call this **neuroplasticity**. When you engage in repeated practice, you literally create new neural pathways.

The more you repeat and refine a skill, the stronger those connections become.

The cool part? Age doesn't matter. Whether you're 16 or 60, your brain can still adapt. The real secret is **consistency.**

Motivation vs. Discipline

Many people start with high motivation, only to lose steam in a few days. That's normal, motivation is designed to spike at the start but fade. Success depends on discipline.

Discipline shows up when motivation doesn't.

In this book, you'll learn simple ways to:

- Make practice automatic.
- Reduce resistance.
- Keep yourself accountable even on low-energy days.

Your Action Step for Today

Write this down somewhere visible:

"Progress over Perfection."

Every skill journey is messy. You'll make mistakes, plateau, and question yourself. That's part of the process. The people who succeed aren't the smartest, they're the ones who keep going.

Quick Recap:

- Your brain is built to learn, at any age.
- Deliberate, focused practice outperforms mindless repetition.
- Motivation gets you started; discipline gets you results.

Ready for Chapter 3?

In the next chapter, we'll map out your 30-day game plan:

- How to break your chosen skill into sub-skills.
- How to set clear, measurable, and motivating goals.
- And how to avoid the most common learning traps.

Let's, ready to dive into Chapter 3!!

3. Designing Your 30-Day Game Plan

"A Goal Without a Plan is Just a Wish"

The difference between those who *hope* to learn something and those who *actually* do is simple:

A clear, structured plan.

This chapter is about setting that plan, so your 30-day journey doesn't depend on willpower or luck, but on strategy.

Step 1: Define Your Why

Before the *how*, comes the *why*.

Ask yourself:

"Why do I want to master this skill?"

A strong reason is your fuel on tough days. Here are some examples:

- "I want to speak Spanish so I can travel confidently this summer."

- "I want to code so I can build my own website."

- "I want to improve my public speaking to grow my career."

When your "why" is clear, excuses become powerless.

Step 2: Break the Skill into Sub-Skills

All big skills are made of smaller parts.

Example:

Want to learn guitar?

Break it down:

1. Chord transitions

2. Strumming patterns

3. Tuning and maintenance

4. Reading tabs

5. Playing simple songs

Want to learn public speaking?

1. Writing a clear speech

2. Voice modulation

3. Body language

4. Handling questions

5. Managing stage anxiety

Sub-skills give you focus. Each day, you'll target one, rather than feeling overwhelmed by the "big picture."

Step 3: Create a 30-Day Roadmap

Now split your practice time across the month:

Days	Focus
Days 1–3	Overview & Sub-skill Mapping
Days 4–10	Foundational Sub-Skills
Days 11–20	Deep Practice + Feedback
Days 21–29	Real-World Application & Refinement
Day 30	Final Review & Celebration

For each day, answer these:

1. **What will I practice today?**

2. **How long will I practice?**

3. **How will I measure progress?**

Step 4: Schedule a Fixed Time

If it's not on your calendar, it won't happen.

Choose:

- **When** you will practice (example: 7-8 AM or 8-9 PM).

- **Where** you will practice (quiet room, library, gym, etc.).

- **How** you will start (set a trigger, e.g., after morning coffee).

Small decisions make a big difference.

Step 5: Track Progress Daily

Tracking progress boosts motivation.

You can use:

- A simple notebook.

- A digital tool (Google Sheets, Trello, Notion).

- A habit tracker app.

Record:

- What you practiced.

- What went well.

- What needs adjustment.

This turns your learning into a feedback loop, the secret to fast improvement.

Step 6: Pre-Commit to Day 30

On **Day 30**, you'll test yourself.

Decide now:

- Will you record yourself performing the skill?

- Will you present it to a friend or coach?

- Will you use it in a real-world situation?

This target gives you clarity. It shifts your mindset from "practice for the sake of practice" to "practice for performance."

Your Action Steps Today

1. Write down your chosen skill.

2. Break it into sub-skills.

3. Fill out this statement:

"I will practice [Skill] for [X] minutes each day at [Time] in [Location]."

4. Mark Day 30 on your calendar as your "Showcase Day."

Key Takeaway:

Mastery is a system, not a secret.

The clearer your plan, the easier your success.

Next Up: Chapter 4

In the next chapter, we'll focus on:

- Building bulletproof habits.

- Beating procrastination.

- Making learning automatic.

4. Turning Practice into a Daily Habit

"You don't rise to the level of your goals — you fall to the level of your systems."- *James Clear*

Motivation gets you started, but habits keep you going.

In this chapter, you'll learn how to set up your practice routine so it feels automatic, even on lazy, busy, or tired days.

The Habit Loop

Every habit is built around a simple cycle:

1. **Cue**: A trigger that reminds you to start.

2. **Routine**: The action (practicing your skill).

3. **Reward**: A feeling of satisfaction or a small reward that locks the habit in.

For example:

Cue: After your morning coffee.

Routine: 30 minutes of guitar practice.

Reward: Listening to your favorite song or checking off a box on your tracker.

Once you repeat this cycle for a few days, your brain starts doing it on autopilot.

Designing Your Practice Habit

Here's a simple formula:

After [Current Habit], I will [New Skill Practice] at [Place] for [Time].

Examples:

- After brushing my teeth, I will practice Spanish flashcards at my desk for 20 minutes.

- After finishing work, I will code for 30 minutes in the study room.

- After dinner, I will do 15 minutes of public speaking drills.

Make It Too Easy to Fail

When starting, aim for **consistency, not intensity**. The golden rule: **"2-Minute Rule"**, make the habit so easy, you can't say no.

Example:

- "I'll practice one chord transition."

- "I'll write one paragraph in Spanish."

- "I'll do one coding exercise."

Once you start, you usually end up doing more. Starting is the hard part, not continuing.

Handling Resistance and Bad Days

There will be days you don't feel like it. That's normal. Here's how to stay on track:

1. **Reduce friction:**

   Keep your tools ready. Guitar on a stand. Laptop open. Flashcards on your desk.

2. **Lower the bar:**

   Bad day? Do *something small* rather than skip entirely. "One page is better than zero."

3. **Use accountability:**

   Tell a friend, join an online community, or post daily updates. External accountability fuels internal discipline.

Micro-Wins = Motivation

Don't wait 30 days to celebrate. Build momentum by recognizing tiny wins:

- First time you memorize 20 new words.

- First time you play a full song.

- First successful mini-project.

Each win rewires your brain to believe:

"I can do this."

Your Action Steps Today

1. Choose your **cue:**

   "I will practice after [habit]."

2. Prepare your **environment:**

   Clear workspace, tools ready.

3. Decide on a **bare minimum:**

   On tough days, you'll do at least [2-5 minutes] of practice.

4. Create a **reward:**

Small celebration after practice i.e. coffee, music, stretching, anything that makes you feel good.

Key Takeaway:

Motivation is great for Day 1.

Habits are great for Day 2 through Day 30.

Your environment, systems, and consistency will carry you to mastery, not willpower.

Next Up: Chapter 5

In the next chapter, you'll learn:

- How to get real-time feedback on your practice.
- How to spot mistakes early (and fix them fast).
- How to use "deliberate practice" to double your learning speed.

5. The Secret to Rapid Growth: Feedback & Deliberate Practice

"Practice doesn't make perfect. Perfect practice makes perfect."

-Vince Lombardi

You've got your routine. You've started showing up. Great. But here's the truth: **just doing the thing isn't enough.** If you want real progress, you need one more ingredient: feedback.

Why Feedback is Your Fastest Teacher

Most people repeat the same mistakes over and over, not because they don't practice, but because no one (or nothing) shows them what to fix.

Feedback shines a light on your blind spots.

The sooner you spot a mistake; the sooner you can correct it.

Two Types of Feedback

1. **Immediate Feedback**

   o   Happens in real-time as you practice.

   o   Example: Playing a song on the guitar, you can hear if the note is wrong.

2. **Delayed Feedback**

   o   Comes after the session, often from others.

   o   Example: A coach reviewing your speech video. A language app grading your pronunciation.

Both are powerful. But using them together is where real growth happens.

What is Deliberate Practice?

Psychologist Anders Ericsson coined the term **deliberate practice**, which means:

- Practicing with full attention.

- Focusing on the *weakest part* of the skill.

- Using feedback to make fast adjustments.

- Repeating until mastery.

Most people just practice what they already know, that feels comfortable but leads to plateaus.

Deliberate practice = discomfort + correction + repetition.

How to Build Feedback Into Your Daily Practice

1. Self-Feedback

- Record yourself (video, audio, code, writing).

- Review it the same day.

- Look for one thing to improve, not ten.

2. Peer Feedback

- Join communities: online forums, local groups, study buddies.

- Post your work, ask:

"What's one thing I could improve?"

3. Expert Feedback

- Hire a coach or take structured feedback from a mentor.

- Often, even a single expert suggestion can save you weeks of trial-and-error.

Warning: Avoid the Comfort Trap

Your brain loves comfort. After the first few days of practice, you'll naturally want to:

- Repeat what you're good at.

- Avoid the parts that feel awkward or difficult.

But growth only happens in the uncomfortable zone. Every time you fix a weakness; you unlock a new level.

Your Action Plan for Today

1. Set up a **feedback loop**:

"I will [record / share / review] my work after every practice session."

2. Find a **feedback partner**:

Ask a friend, coach, or online group to give you weekly feedback.

3. Schedule **feedback days**:

Once a week, review all your practice, identify patterns, and make corrections.

Key Takeaway:

Practice makes habits.

Deliberate practice makes mastery.

Feedback isn't criticism, it's your personal GPS for faster learning.

Next Up: Chapter 6

In the next chapter, we'll focus on:

- How to apply your skill in real-world situations.

- Why "using" the skill is the real test of learning.

- How to transform practice into true confidence.

6. Practice Meets Reality: Applying Your Skill

"Knowledge is of no value unless you put it into practice."

-Anton Chekhov

Practicing a skill in isolation is one thing.

But applying it in real life? That's when your growth skyrockets.

This chapter is about moving from practice mode to real-world action, where confidence is born.

Why Application is the Real Test

- It's easy to memorize grammar rules.

- It's harder to hold a conversation with a native speaker.

- It's easy to practice guitar chords in your room.

- It's harder to play a song in front of someone.

Application exposes gaps, sharpens your reflexes, and builds real confidence.
It's where your brain switches from "I've practiced this" to "I own this."

The Skill Ladder

Level	Description	Example
Practice	Controlled environment. Low pressure.	Rehearsing a speech alone.
Simulation	Slightly realistic scenario. Mid pressure.	Practicing a mock speech with a friend.
Application	Real environment. High stakes.	Giving the speech at an event.

Most people get stuck between Practice and Simulation.
Real growth happens when you push into **Application Mode**.

Real-World Practice Ideas

No matter what skill you're learning, you can create real-life exposure:

Skill	Real-World Application
Language	Have a daily conversation with a native speaker online (e.g., HelloTalk, iTalki).
Public Speaking	Join a local Toastmasters club, speak at events or open-mic nights.
Coding	Build and launch a small app or website.
Photography	Do a photo challenge and publish on social media.
Cooking	Host a dinner for friends or family.

Why Real-World Pressure Is Good

When you practice under real-world conditions:

- Your brain learns to handle pressure.

- Your weaknesses are revealed faster.

- Your skill becomes resilient and automatic.

You won't feel "ready" the first time. That's normal. The secret?
Do it before you feel ready. Growth always follows action.

Action Steps for Real-World Application

1. **Pick a real-world event**

Book it. Sign up. Announce it. Put it on your calendar.
Make the commitment public if possible.

2. **Simulate the experience**

Practice as close to the real situation as you can.
Example: Give your speech to a friend standing at a distance, record it,
and watch it back.

3. **Debrief & Reflect**

After every real-world application, ask:

- What went well?

- What felt hard?

- What would I change for next time?

Key Takeaway:

Practice gives you knowledge.
Application builds mastery.

Real progress starts the moment you apply your skill in the wild, imperfectly, awkwardly, but bravely.

Coming Up: Chapter 7

In the next chapter, we'll cover:

- How to reflect on your progress.

- How to avoid "skill decay."

- How to build on your 30-day success so you keep growing.

7. Reflect, Refine, and Reinforce

"We do not learn from experience... we learn from reflecting on experience."- *John Dewey*

Congratulations!! you've been showing up, practicing deliberately, and applying your skill in real life. That's huge.

But the real secret to long-term mastery isn't just practice.
It's **reflection, refinement, and reinforcement.**

This chapter will help you lock in what you've learned — and make sure you don't lose it.

Why Reflection Accelerates Growth

Without reflection, mistakes get repeated. Progress plateaus. Motivation fades.

With reflection, you:

- Notice what's working.

- Spot patterns.

- Avoid wasted effort.

A 5-minute review after practice can save you 5 hours of repeating the same errors.

The Daily Reflection Formula

Here's a simple journal prompt to use after every session:

1. **What did I practice today?**
   (e.g. "Worked on strumming patterns, focused on speed.")

2. **What went well?**
   (e.g. "My transitions between chords felt smoother.")

3. **What felt hard?**
   (e.g. "Struggled to keep consistent tempo.")

4. **What will I adjust tomorrow?**
   (e.g. "Slow down tempo and use a metronome.")

This habit transforms your practice from "going through the motions" to "intentional learning."

The Weekly Review

At the end of each week, zoom out:

- What sub-skills have improved?

- What still needs work?

- Have I applied the skill in real life this week?

- Did I stay consistent with practice time and focus?

This review will show whether your plan needs tweaking, or whether you're right on track.

Avoiding Skill Decay

Skills are like muscles.
If you stop using them, they shrink.

After your 30-day sprint, don't let the habit die! Here's how to keep your skill sharp:

1. **Maintenance Sessions**
   Even 15 minutes, 3-4 times a week, prevents decay.

2. **Teach Someone Else**
   Teaching forces deep understanding — the ultimate reinforcement.

3. **Set a New Challenge**
   Once the 30 days are up, pick a slightly harder goal.

Example:
If you've learned basic Spanish conversations in 30 days, aim to write a short essay or have a 30-minute chat with a native speaker.

Reinforcement is a Loop, Not a Finish Line

Mastery isn't a one-time achievement.
It's a loop:

Practice → Feedback → Reflection → Application → Repeat

The more you run the loop, the more skilled you become.

Your Action Steps Today

1. **Start a Reflection Habit**

Use the Daily Reflection Formula for every practice session this week.

2. **Schedule a Weekly Review**

Choose one day (Sunday is ideal) to review your progress.

3. **Plan Your Post-30-Day Challenge**

Write down one next-level goal for the skill you're working on.

Key Takeaway:

The fastest learners aren't just the hardest workers.
They're the most reflective.

Mastery is built in the pauses, as much as in the practice.

Coming Up: Chapter 8

The final chapter will tie everything together:

- How to sustain lifelong learning.

- How to stack new skills once you've mastered one.

- How to stay curious and unstoppable.

8. Beyond 30 Days: The Lifelong Skill-Building Formula

"Once you stop learning, you start dying."

-Albert Einstein

So here you are. You've practiced. You've applied. You've reflected.

But the truth is: **this isn't the end — it's just the beginning**.

Mastering a skill in 30 days isn't a finish line.
It's proof that you can do it, and now, you can repeat the process for anything.

The Growth Loop Never Ends

The world belongs to lifelong learners.

Here's the loop you've built over the past month:

Curiosity → Commitment → Practice → Feedback → Reflection → Real-World Application → Mastery → Curiosity (again)

Once you complete this cycle once, it becomes easier to:

- Pick up new skills.

- Level up old ones.

- Stay flexible in a fast-changing world.

Stacking Skills = Exponential Growth

Single skills are powerful.
But **stacked skills** are game-changing.

Example:

Core Skill	Complementary Skills	Superpower Outcome
Public Speaking	Storytelling + Persuasion	Powerful leader or educator
Coding	Design + UX thinking	Build complete apps
Writing	Marketing + SEO	Build an audience, sell ideas

When you stack skills together, your value in any field multiplies.
Skill 1 + Skill 2 + Skill 3 = Unstoppable You.

Mindset Shift: From "Goal-Setter" to "Skill-Builder"

Most people set goals like:

- "I want to lose 10 kg."

- "I want to earn X money."

- "I want to speak Spanish."

But successful learners shift their thinking:

"Who do I need to become?"
 "What skills would that person have?"
"How can I practice them every day?"

Focusing on skills — not just outcomes — makes the process fun, motivating, and long-lasting.

The Skill Flywheel

Once you master one skill, the next becomes easier.

1st Skill	2nd Skill	3rd Skill	Lifelong Learning Becomes:
Hard	Easier	Natural	Part of who you are.

Because you've learned **how** to learn.

That's the real prize of your 30-day challenge.

Celebrate Progress, Not Perfection

Mastery isn't about being the best.
It's about being better than yesterday.

Celebrate:

- Every mistake you learned from.

- Every small win.

- The fact that you didn't give up.

Progress = happiness.
Perfection = frustration.

Your Action Steps for Lifelong Growth

1. Choose your **next skill**.

What's something new you've always wanted to learn?

2. Use the **30-Day Game Plan**.

The same structure you used here will help you tackle it.

3. Keep a **Skill Journal**.

Log each new skill and track your growth year after year.

Final Thoughts: You Are a Learner for Life

You've proven you can learn anything, in 30 days or less.

No one can take that away from you.

Now, the only limit is your curiosity.

Your Skill-Building Mantra:

"I am not born with fixed talents.
I am built by daily practice, feedback, and action."

Repeat that anytime self-doubt creeps in.

The End, and The Beginning

Master Any Skill in 30 Days isn't just a book.
It's a blueprint for the rest of your life.

The world changes fast. New opportunities arrive every day.
And now you know:

No matter what skill you choose, you can master it.

Conclusion: Your 30-Day Transformation

In just 30 days, you've proven that learning isn't about talent. It's about action, commitment, and mindset.

The tools are now in your hands:

- Set a clear, meaningful goal.
- Break it down into daily practice.
- Use feedback and reflection to adjust.
- Apply the skill in real life.
- Celebrate progress, not perfection.

The only real failure is giving up.
The only real limit is the story you tell yourself.

From this moment on, you're no longer a "beginner."
You're a **lifelong learner**, and that makes you unstoppable.

Bonus: The 30-Day Mastery Checklist

Post this on your wall, desk, or device and check off every day:

Day	Practiced	Got Feedback	Reflected	Applied Skill
1	☐	☐	☐	☐
2	☐	☐	☐	☐
3	☐	☐	☐	☐
...	...	...	...	...
30	☐	☐	☐	☐

If you miss a day: No guilt, just restart the next day.
Progress is never a straight line, it's a cycle.

Your Mastery Affirmation:
"I can learn anything, if I give myself the time, focus, and space to practice."